SPORTING 🏆 HEROES

FARA WILLIAMS

ROY APPS

ILLUSTRATED BY ALESSANDRO VALDRIGHI

LONDON·SYDNEY

Franklin Watts
First published in Great Britain in 2017
by The Watts Publishing Group

Text © Roy Apps 2017
Illustrations © Watts Publishing Group 2017
Cover design: Peter Scoulding
Executive Editor: Adrian Cole

*The statistics in this book were correct at the time
of printing, but because of the nature of the sport,
it cannot be guaranteed that they are now accurate.*

HB ISBN 978 1 4451 5326 1
PB ISBN 978 1 4451 5329 2
Library ebook ISBN 978 1 4451 5327 8

1 3 5 7 9 10 8 6 4 2

Printed in China

Franklin Watts
An imprint of
Hachette Children's Group
Part of The Watts Publishing Group
Carmelite House
50 Victoria Embankment
London EC4Y 0DZ

An Hachette UK Company
www.hachette.co.uk

www.franklinwatts.co.uk

FARA WAITED FOR HER MUM TO SAY SOMETHING, BUT SHE DIDN'T.

FARA HAD NOWHERE TO GO. SHE WAS JUST SEVENTEEN YEARS OLD.

ALL SHE HAD WITH HER WERE A FEW CLOTHES, A LITTLE BIT OF MONEY AND HER MOST TREASURED POSSESSION...

...HER FOOTBALL BOOTS.

CHAPTER TWO
ON THE STREETS

It was scary. Lonely. On the streets at night.

A lot of the other homeless people around her had cans of drink with them. To Fara, they seemed sick, crazy even. There were noises everywhere. Cars and taxis hooting, buses revving, people calling out and shouting.

One night, while she was curled up under the arches down by the river, an old guy came and sat down beside her.

'Haven't seen you down here before,' he said.

Fara shook her head. The old man spoke in an educated voice.

'Everyone looks a bit scary, don't they? Acting mad; screaming their heads off ... it's a good way to stop people coming near you. People who might do you harm — and I'm not talking about other homeless people. I mean the general public.'

'Harm you?' Fara asked.

'Yeah. The worst time is after the pubs kick out,' he said.

'Oh,' Fara said, nervously. 'If you don't mind me saying, you seem a bit posh to be homeless.'

The man shrugged. 'I had a good job, nice house, wife and family once. Then, I was made redundant. Lost the house. My wife left with the kids. I had nothing. That's how I ended up here.' He looked hard at the football boots Fara was clutching.

'Nice boots. Do you play?'

Fara nodded. 'For Chelsea Ladies.'

The man raised his eyebrows. 'Are you any good?'

'I've scored 16 goals this season so far.'

'That is good. And it's even better that you've got something you're talented at. It'll give you a chance to get off the streets. When's your next match?'

'Tomorrow night.'

The man struggled to his feet. He moved away. 'Make sure you score a hat-trick!' he called.

Fara curled up beneath two large sheets of cardboard. She needed to get some sleep. She had a big match tomorrow.

CHAPTER THREE
FINDING HOPE

Fara told nobody at Chelsea Ladies that she was homeless. She would simply turn up for training or for a match and play her heart out.

Her goal-scoring exploits had not gone unnoticed at national level though, and she had made a good impression playing for the England Under-19s.

Not long after she had left home, Fara spent a week training with the England Under-19 squad. The team all stayed in a hotel for the week. It was hard work, but Fara enjoyed it.

They had been training with Hope Powell, who managed the England Women's senior team.

The end of the week came all too soon. As well as the football, Fara had enjoyed sleeping in a bed again. If she had realised just how bad living on the streets was, she would never have left home.

Fara wondered if she should go back home. But, no, she thought. It would be just as bad as before, if not worse. They would think they had won.

'You all right, Fara?' one of her teammates asked, when they caught her daydreaming.

Fara shrugged. 'Oh, fine.' She still hadn't told anybody that she was living on the streets. She was too ashamed.

Fara watched her teammates go their various ways. She hung about on the hotel steps wondering what to do with herself before it was time to make her

way to the railway arches down
by the river. A car pulled up. It was
Hope Powell.

'Can I give you a lift home, Fara? You
live in Battersea, don't you? That's not
far out of my way. Hop in.'

Fara climbed into the passenger seat.
She sighed. There was no way she could
keep her homelessness a secret now.
'I don't live at home any more. I had
a big row with my mum and auntie.'

'Where are you staying then?' asked
Hope.

Fara shrugged. 'Oh, you know. Here
and there...'

Hope looked hard at Fara. 'You're
homeless, aren't you?'

Fara nodded, slowly.

'There's no shame in being homeless,' Hope said, quietly. 'Listen, my mum used to take in foster kids. A lot of them had fallen out with people at home. But you can't go on sleeping on the streets. For one thing it's dangerous. And for another thing, you need to be sleeping properly if you're going to be any good for me in the England squad.'

'I'm not going back home,' said Fara.

'No, you're coming with me,' replied Hope. 'There's a homeless person's shelter I know up by King's Cross.'

She stopped the car, turned it round and drove back up through the city of London towards King's Cross.

CHAPTER FOUR
MEETING MO

Once Fara was settled into the homeless shelter, Hope bought her a sleeping bag.

'The sheets and blankets here are clean,' she explained. 'But it's good to have a decent sleeping bag you can call your own.'

In 2001, just a few months after moving into the homeless shelter, Fara made her full England debut. She came on as a substitute against Portugal during the World Cup qualifier at Fratton Park.

She played for England again in the return match the following February. With the score 0—0, England won a free kick. Fara took it; curling the ball up and over the wall, and past the

Portuguese goalkeeper. It was her first goal for England.

That same season, Fara moved from Chelsea to Charlton Athletic Ladies. She won the club's Player of the Year Award and the FA Women's Young Player of the Year Award.

Fara moved out of the homeless shelter to a hostel. She still had nowhere she thought of as home, though.

Fara was into her third season with Charlton Athletic, when the team travelled up to Liverpool to play against Everton Ladies.

After the match, Fara found the Everton manager, Mo Marley, waiting to talk to her...

ONE DAY, AFTER TRAINING...

YOU SHOULD GET YOUR OWN FLAT UP HERE.

I'D LOVE TO, MO. BUT I CAN'T AFFORD IT.*

YOU COULD IF YOU HAD A JOB. EVERTON NEEDS A COMMUNITY COACH TO WORK WITH YOUNG FOOTBALLERS IN SCHOOLS AND YOUTH CLUBS.

FARA MOVED UP TO LIVERPOOL. SHE HAD A NEW TEAM, A PAYING JOB – AND BEST OF ALL, SHE HAD A HOME AT LAST.

*Most women players were not paid a living wage by their club at this time.

CHAPTER FIVE
MISSING MUM

With her new job and home, Fara found herself on top form. Everton fans nicknamed her 'Queen Fara'.

She was also fast becoming a star of the England team. In 2007, she received the FA International Player of the Year Award. In 2008, she scored her first England hat-trick; three spectacular, long-range goals against Belarus.

FARA WILLIAMS HAS THE BALL...
IT'S A SUPERB STRIKE! THAT'S
HER HAT-TRICK!

One day, Fara got a phone call from her cousin.

'Got some sad news, Fara. Grandad's died.'

'Oh no...'

'Will you be coming to the funeral?'

'Yes, of course.'

All of Fara's family was at the funeral, including her mum. Fara passed her on their way into the church, but neither of them spoke.

Afterwards, Fara's mind was in turmoil.

'Mum should've spoken to me. She should've apologised for not standing up for me when my aunt threw me out! I guess she's too proud and too stubborn...

…a bit like me really.'

Time drifted by. Fara thought about her mum every day.

In 2009, England were playing Italy in the Women's European Championships. England won a penalty. Fara stepped up to take it. Her thunderous shot rocketed past Italy's goalkeeper.

As her teammates mobbed her, Fara reached up and made the shape of a heart with her hand. She didn't know it, but her mum was watching the match on TV and saw Fara make the sign.

What Fara didn't know either, was that her mum had her phone number. Her mum wrote a short text message and hit SEND.

Fara's heart skipped a beat. Suppose her aunt was still with her mum, waiting to shout and scream at her again? Suppose her mum was going to tell her off for leaving home? In a blind panic she hit DELETE. Another ping, and the message and the number were both gone from her screen.

Straight away Fara regretted what she had done.

'How could I be so stubborn! Why didn't I answer the message?' she thought. But it was too late. She hoped that her mum would call. But the phone remained silent. Now, all she could do was lie down on her bed and cry herself to sleep.

CHAPTER SIX
THE MESSAGE

Fara focused on her football, but barely a day went by without her thinking of her mum. In the semi-final of the 2010 FA Women's Cup, Fara scored against her old club, Chelsea. In the final she helped Everton win the trophy, as they beat Arsenal 3—2 after extra time.

2011 - WORLD CUP QUALIFIER: ENGLAND VS SWITZERLAND.

PWEEEEEEEEP!

IT'S A PENALTY! WILLIAMS STEPS UP...

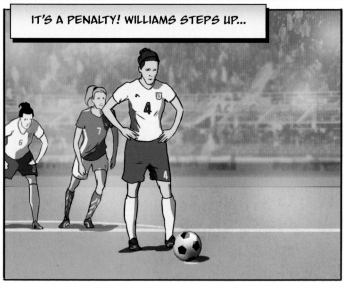

30

As the team celebrated in their hotel after the game, Fara checked her phone. The first text was from her mum. This time she didn't delete it.

Fara slipped away to be alone in her hotel room. She sat down and read her mum's message:

> Thanks for the goal: 50th minute
> and 2 days before my 50th birthday!
> Miss you. Luv Mum ♥♥

Fara sniffed back a tear, smiled to herself and texted her mum back:

> Thanks Mum. I've missed you too.

Then, Fara went back downstairs to celebrate with her teammates: not just the fact that England were through to the finals of the Euros, but also because she knew deep down that soon she would be reunited with her mum.

CHAPTER SEVEN
MEETING MUM

Fara arranged to meet her mum at a coffee shop. She got there early — afraid that her mum would leave if she didn't see Fara waiting to meet her.

Fara sat looking at the door, watching people come in. Then, a middle-aged woman stood in the doorway. Fara recognised her straight away, even after nine years apart.

'Mum!'

She waved to her. Suddenly, they were both smiling and crying at the same time. They didn't say a word to each other; they just hugged.

THEY SAT DOWN WITH THEIR DRINKS.

NOW, LET'S TALK ABOUT THE IMPORTANT STUFF.

IMPORTANT STUFF...?

Fara's mum laughed. 'Football, of course! How are England going to do in the Women's World Cup? Is your team, Everton, going to win the league?'

'I didn't know you liked football, Mum.'

'I didn't. But when you left home, I followed your career. Every time England Women have been on the TV, I've been watching.'

'But you've never been to a match?'

Fara's mum shook her head. 'No, I didn't want you to see me in the crowd and be put off.'

Fara chatted with her mum until it was time for her to go back to Liverpool.

Leaving was hard, but Fara knew that she would see her mum again soon, now that they had put the past behind them.

CHAPTER EIGHT
MOST CAPPED

In 2012, Fara left Everton and signed for local rivals Liverpool. In her first season, she helped them win the 2013 Women's Super League title.

A year later, in August 2014, Fara led the England Women team out against Sweden. It was her 130th cap — she was now the most capped player in English football history.

Fara's mum continued to be her biggest fan. She texted her congratulations to Fara. Fara called her back.

'Hey, Mum. Fancy watching England at Wembley?'

'Will Stevie Gerrard be playing?' Steven Gerrard was her mum's second favourite player, after Fara.

'No, I will! England Women are playing at Wembley for the first time ever!'

In November 2014, a crowd of over 45,000 watched England — with Fara Williams at the centre of midfield — play Germany. The crowd was noisy, but above the shouting and chanting, Fara was sure she could hear one proud voice above all the rest:

'Come on, Fara! That's my girl!'

CHAPTER NINE

WORLD CUP GLORY

It was a great moment for Fara, playing at Wembley in front of an enthusiastic crowd that included her mum.

There was one disappointing thing though: Germany, not England, won the friendly match, with the final score 3—0.

Fara, and the rest of the team, were determined to put that right.

The next time England played Germany was in the 2015 FIFA Women's World Cup. The match would decide who got the bronze medal for third place. It was a tense, hard-fought game. The ref blew for full-time with the score at 0—0.

After the first period of extra time it was still 0—0.

Then, three minutes into the second period of extra time, the German defender Kemme brought down England's Lianne Sanderson in the box.

'PENALTY!'

Fara placed the ball on the spot. The crowd was absolutely silent. Fara could feel her heart beating fast and hear the blood pounding in her head. She stepped up, shot...

'GOAL!'

It was enough. With Fara Williams's goal, England won the match 1—0, and with it third place in the World Cup. It was the best performance at a finals by any England football team in forty-nine years.

CHAPTER TEN
WEMBLEY WINNER

Wednesday 22nd January 2016 was a typically dull winter's day in London. None of that bothered Fara — this was the proudest day of her life. She was going to Buckingham Palace to receive an MBE from Princess Anne.

It was a very special way to start a new year, and a new chapter in her footballing career. Two weeks before, she had tweeted her followers:

> It is now time for a new
> chapter and I am delighted to
> join @ArsenalLadies for the next
> two years!!

Living back in London, Fara missed Liverpool; her house, her friends, the fans.

But Fara soon settled into the Arsenal set-up, and the team benefitted from her experience. In the 2016 FA Cup semi-final against Sunderland, Arsenal were awarded a penalty. Fara stepped up...

One step. Two steps. Kick. GOAL! Arsenal headed through to the final!

A record crowd of nearly 32,000 watched the Cup Final at Wembley between

Arsenal and Chelsea. Arsenal took an early lead, but Chelsea were strong and fought hard. It took a huge effort from Fara in midfield to help win the match.

The Arsenal defence held strong. Final score: Arsenal 1—0 Chelsea.

It was Fara's first FA Women's Cup Winner's medal since 2010. Her move to Arsenal had certainly paid off.

FACT FILE

Full name: Fara Tanya Franki Williams Merrett

Nickname: Queen Fara

Date of birth: 25th January 1984

Place of birth: London, England

Height: 1.64m (5ft 4in)

GLOSSARY

Fratton Park — home ground of Portsmouth FC

hat-trick — three goals scored by the same player in one match

maturity — performing in a grown-up way

MBE — Member of the Order of the British Empire — awarded for outstanding achievement or service to the community

redundant — no longer needed

stubborn — when someone doesn't want to change an action or view; headstrong

substitute — a player who comes on during a match in place of another player

CAREER

Trophies won at Charlton:

FA Women's Premier League Cup	2003—04

Trophies won at Everton:

FA Women's Premier League Cup	2007—08
FA Women's Cup	2010

Trophies won at Liverpool:

FA Women's Super League	2013 and 2014

Trophies won at Arsenal:

FA Women's Cup	2016

International Trophies:

Cyprus Cup	2009, 2013, 2015

Individual Honours

FA International Women's Player of the Year	2006—07 and 2008—09
FA Women's Players' Player of the Year	2008—09
FA Women's Young Player of the Year	2001—02
PFA Women's Team of the Year	2013—14

Records

3rd August 2014 — became the most capped England Women's player

For the 11-year-old Neymar, playing and training with Santos FC Academy was like being in another world.

For a start, it was a big club, one of only five never to have been relegated from the Brazilian top-tier of football.

One day, Neymar was told, 'Another club wants to have a look at you.'

'A big club?' asked Neymar.

'They don't get much bigger than this. Real Madrid want to give you a trial...'

CONTINUE READING
NEYMAR'S
AMAZING STORY IN...

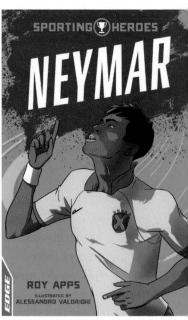